Before
We Remember
We Dream

BRYAN THAO WORRA

Dedicated to the ones
who taught me,
and the ones
who stood by me.

And K.

Vientiane in 12 Haikus

1.

Sandalwood city
The moon hangs high above us
Night fragrant and calm.

2.

So many temples here,
Monuments and kind people
The Buddha strolls by.

3.

See the Talaat Sao,
How the Morning Market grew.
We trade first moments.

4.

Quiet history,
Pristine Eden, paradise
Between civil wars.

5.

Climb the Patuxai
Honoring veterans here:
An arch, a fine view.

6.

Doctors and nurses,
Old Mahosot Hospital.
Health and Sabaidees.

7.

Mattie and Chris film
Ghost movies and other stories,
A sleepy whippet

8.

No giant monsters
Have been seen here in ages
Ah, how they slumber!

9.

My family left
Years ago, but, oh, memories,
Seeking each other.

10.

If you come visit,
Have a BeerLao by the shore.
Dear Mekong, khop jai.

11.

Circle That Luang
Making merit, remembering
Those who came before.

12.

When you depart home:
On the Wattay tarmac, wish,
And you might return.

Narrative of the Nak's Heirs

Never read my life
As the diary of some sad refugee.

My account is not intended
As a routine narrative of adversity overcome,
"Mere survival" once again, transcending
A descent to White-Hot Hell
Converted to the Placid Limbo of Frogs.

Know I miss the familiar strange here,
In a way you cannot fathom.

Our hard ghosts remain vigilant,
Thin as an inked scratch on an old palm leaf
Haunting with a tongue claimed incomprehensible.

The old signposts have been lost,
But in strangeness, possibility.

I hope, moving, a shadow in uncertain passages
Making melodies for newsless souls.
In daring this, might I shape some limitless star?

We, scrambling to replace what we barely knew,
Barely recognize our tangled metamorphosis,
Our hymns of recovery organs of uncertain purpose
In the body cosmic, mistaken easily

For endings, not new beginnings.

Oriental Rat Flea

You've known pyramids and paupers,
Vermin and saints, filling graveyards
Between your leaps with your mouth
Of plagues for every age and eon.

Who brought you so far to Olympus,
Xenopsylla cheopis, now made immortal
In your impossible, improbable diaspora,
But still a mote in our boundless cosmos.

Among these mighty pens and laurels,
These songs of fading gods and apocalypse,

What do you know of Vientiane or Versailles,
Vincent Chin, Mekong deltas or fabled Delphi?

Yet a single bite can rouse legendary lions
Whose roars might move a thousand stars
The way mere butterflies level vast empires

.

For all of this, I gaze with you at the distant peaks
Of Mt. Meru a cosmic ocean, a lifetime away,
    Scratching with a sigh, an unspeakable memory.

Phnom Penh in January

In the old country,
My friend is amazed
At the tiny silver boxes
Arrayed in the market square
Ornate rows, tight-lipped and cryptic.

"They look like coffins for inchworms,"
She jests.

I tell her they're for betel nuts.

"Great for intestinal worms,"
Or so the spitting elders tell us,
Petting their bellies of hollow.

 We went to grab some vermicelli,
Passing what looked like

     A   freshly   quartered   manta

In a bamboo basket on the way
His pale lips mouthing
Dark pronouncements on us all
His tail flicking on a squalid table,
Waving goodbye at the many tourists

In these markets of carcass
Every bite becomes a postcard
Colorful as saffron monks
Smoking in the street

On the Road to Vientiane, 1975

Bad enough the secret city fell
In a secret war with human faces.
A road of refugees making their run for it:
Some strange hopes prevailed, frantic,
    Littering the way with filth and stragglers
           Discarding a thousand things
   They'd been so certain they'd need.
There was a major I knew escorting them,
Sent to keep something   close to order
    At   the end.

By the roadside he recognized two men.
    He'd grown up with them,
              Attended one's wedding.
In their despair, with old knives,
      They'd slit each other's bellies open,
Trying to get a taste of opium
   In the other's warm fat.

The air reeked of bowels and defeat.
He left them behind that day to die
As such men die in the Laotian dust.

But thirty years later in Minnesota,
He still remembers their eyes
When they offered to cut him open, too.

Riding the Tiger

Burying my wars, these memories of you:
"It don't mean nothing," wondering who
Will stop the rain and who knows the way back
To San Jose, ten thousand places you left your hearts.
What a song for all of these waters and slaughters.

It seems almost unthinkable but I'll ask anyway:
In the shadows of Saigon in your olive and pomp,
Did you really see yourselves in your rumbling array
As some smiling lady rider from Niger
Or believe you were merely the tiger?

All of this napalm, the burning bright,
Our fearful symmetries, these roaring hogs,
Hurling yourselves at the moon and stars,
Striped Liberty gorging with impunity, weapons free,

You came a long way, babies, for hearts and minds.
Lighting huts like there's a snazzy medal down the avenue,
You never pause to think what it really means to come back,
Deep down inside, from this land of cyclos and samsara,
Snickering at weretiger rumors,

      Shining bullets for a voracious phoenix.

Déjà vu

Ken Burns is bringing up the Vietnam War,
It's a documentary with a soundtrack to die for:
Nine Inch Nails and Yo Yo Ma, Ray Charles and CCR.
18 hours to cover a war of 20 years and 180 days.
Or 19 years, depending on who you ask, picking up
Shortly after the end of the French at Dien Bien Phu.

For the occasion,
I filmed a poem of mine this summer that someone found again,
One I wrote in 2002 as I remembered a visit in November, 1997
In Missoula among Hmong veterans while searching for my family.
It's a long story.

A poem doesn't give you much time to talk about Secret Wars
Or valkyries, spectres or the secret stories behind the codenames
Of Company men like Hog and Kayak, Black Lion or Mr. Clean.

I hold old photographs in my hand, I click through digital faces
Salvaged from old legionnaire estate sales, dying photographers
Who thought I might like to know what they saw in my lost jungles.
For a price.

It's the closest I get to a time machine, with no way to change
The present, but possibly the future. Still, I've said this to you before.
In writing this, Time stops being a one-way river, less a bamboo Styx.

1,080 minutes is all of the time they think we can spare
Forty years later on a war that never ended for many of us,
Our voices fleeting smoke they try to box into a neat package,
Believed a bygone era we'll never relive again, Buddhist ideas aside.

Missoula, 1976

At 3 years old in Montana,
I became a citizen on Flag Day
During the American bicentennial.

That and a cup of coffee gets you
A cup of coffee even if you write
A thousand poems for a million elephants.

I didn't stay there, of course,
But in this city I met my first ghosts
And dinosaurs, gorgons and ancient gods.

I played with a young girl named Dulcinea,
Discovered the family pigs eaten by a bear,

And saw my first neighbor die,
Crushed beneath a fallen telephone pole.

I wish I remembered his name.

Our family dog Dutch, in his tragic jealousy,
Tried to kill me a few times.
I still have one scar from it after 40 years.

But I miss him anyway,
Because that's the way refugee memory works.

Moving Mountains, Burning Stars

In Germany, the Krupps Bagger-288
Was forged to kill mountains,
Towering 96 meters and 13,500 tons,
Indifferent to poetic subtlety.

This isn't the work of surgeons,
Cutting to a mountain's coal heart,
Maybe an ancient vein of diamonds
Worthy of mortal beauties.
 Watch it cross a road, and you might
Feel more minute than an old man gazing at
The summer mountains of Qu Ding.

Witness it raze some sprawling range,
Dare you feel like a deity, some peer of Vulcan
At his fire who needs no scenery of mere stones?

There are tiny men from Sydney and Beijing
Who smile to eagerly bring such tools
To the peaks of antique Luang Prabang,
Our groves of teak, our sacred caverns and isles.
In a small room in the cosmos, these fleas haggle.
One day, they might reach Mars or Alpha Centauri,
Long after our own foolish names are rightfully lost
Amid flickering stars and cold galactic memory.

Anchorage, 1979

What stuck with me after 38 years likely
Ought to be regarded as refugee trivia.
Minutiae from a fraction of life fragmented.
Anchorage flows back into my memory for reasons
Nebulous as Wendigo howls beneath the Aurora Borealis.

I still dream of Mt. McKinley among the clouds. That moose.
Some fierce Kodiak that towered above me in a mall trophy case
I now see was no bigger than my father, roaring for eternity,
Collecting dust. There was a neighbor who smoked salmon
I still remember as if it was yesterday, that never makes it
To the stores. No words can convey how much
You are missing out, even as I can never taste it again, either.

One reconciles with that.
I probably shouldn't spare a word for that cute little redhead girl
Who bit me on the knee in the doctor's office. The pack
Of young women who taught me the nuances of Alaskan racism
Over a pair of new white shoes. Walking home alone in deep snow
Because classmates told me the bus left without me, when it hadn't.

But I'm not sure how you spelled Pung's name anymore,
Let alone where her journey took her after our secret tropical wars.

For No One In Particular

Please forgive me,

But if I write a poem about you

We won't end up together.

That's just the truth of it,

After three decades.

It's as good a deal as you get,

With a poet from Vientiane.

For my parting gift, please know

I'm returning now to my ten thousand verses

Of the Laopocalypse and all of its unspeakable calamities.

ຈີ Chu

Here, my mouth is an ink waterfall
By the shore of your beautiful body
Of legends.
One day, a hero like Sithong, Sinxay,
Or a wandering wit like Xieng Mieng
Might come upon my modest verses
And fondly remember bustling Market Street
With the same delight as storied Thanon Fa Ngum,
Even if my own momentary name is forgotten
Like the architect of your first Wat
Or the last cook for the Buddha

Ypsilanti, 1982

In 36 years, I barely spared a word
About my days in Ypsilanti,
Known chiefly for giving us Iggy Pop
And an obscure pioneer in continental drift.

I was watching the 9 o'clock news
With my father in our living room,
As was the family habit. I was 9,

Eating a Baby Ruth in June
When a picture of Vincent Chin
Flashed onscreen with a discussion
Of murder, Japan and the Motor City.

My father said not to take it personally.
We were going to have a barbecue with
Our blue collar neighbor on Saturday,
Once he was done at the Ford factory.

Our other neighbor across the way
With the tall bottle-blonde daughters
Was a Baptist preacher, fond of discussing
Pearl Harbor with me every other day,
Because I couldn't tell him a thing about Laos.

The Lady of Lake Yosemite

By her learned bobcats and bovines idly grazing,
Beneath the waters of Lake Yosemite, she's a secret Nakini,
Who hates the graffiti on her solitary spire,
But it dissuades curious tourists and their gazing.

She'll chuckle if you ask her true name,
As Nakini are known to do, full of sacred fire.
She'll hint with a whisper in the long grass,
The lap of a clear wave against the placid shore,
The tumble of a leaf, the scent of a fairy shrimp.

Her sister plays nearby, disguised as a beautiful field
Who might grow one day to become anything.
Wheat for harvest, a spaceport, a grove of almonds,
A vineyard fit for scholars and kings.

Some days she shows up as a mermaid,
A snake in the temple, a playful bee, a beauty.
I tried to take a picture of her for you,

But she knocked my camera over,
Disguised as a laughing gust while it broke,

       Promising if I return, there will be an even better story.

I left behind a bottle of wine for her in a secret place,
Departing Merced with new memories worthy of legend,
At least a thousand poems.

My Secret War Within

The first film in the world
To feature Lao was *Chang*
By the man who would one day
Film *King Kong* with ample Fay Wray.
He never returned to the heirs of Lane Xang,
But he died among New Years and April Fools
In the year I was born, when covert American bombs
Stopped falling
Like steel rain
                Over the Realm of a Million Elephants.
Dr. Dooley played *Dumbo* for us in the hills:
Flying pachyderms and talking crows, useless feathers,
Something about belief,
While Ravens, fans of Poe, dug into the Plain of Jars
And we made our fresh ghosts for the next generation.
I never understood their stories until years later,
When my father, almost dead from a thousand smokes,
Referred to them as heroes,
Pointing to a portrait of a young boy, who could have been
Me, in another un-American lifetime, by these men,
M-16 in hand, smiling for a reporter's camera.
On the edge of Detroit,
I grew up among Godzilla films, the aliens of UHF,
Alarming, relentless, a comfort more family
Than the silent faces of *Apocalypse Now*
Or slinky women who promised love for a long time,
If I understood American dollars and full metal jackets.

My teacher tries to show me *The Joy Luck Club*, *Air America*
"Here is the truth of who you are, surely."
I return to *Alien Nation, Enemy Mine, They Live, The Thing*.

My love says I can't tell my story talking about other people's films.
"No one's seen half of what you watched."

"No one's seen half of what I lived."
I reply, trying to shred my life into ink, just to remain.

Mattie Do made a ghost movie the other day, *Chanthaly*.
Shows me.
We can't talk about half the worlds we've had,
Our wars gone by, her crazed ghosts,
My …

Little Laos on the Prairie Magazine gets a letter, from a man
Who wants to make a movie about our war.
Says he knows a great place to shoot in Hawaii,
Same same, but different, spread the word, send some cash.
He has a cause, his special vision, if not the facts.
I lost his number, and cast my father's ashes into the Mississippi.

The last I heard,
He now wished he'd spoken to assassins, instead.

Secrets of Lao Super Science

It's a badly kept secret Ajahn Dao's equation
Rivals E=mc2, relatively speaking, at least in Vientiane.

It's marginally less frustrating than Fermat's last theorem
But certainly goes beyond that mathematical python a2 + b2 = c2

It won't upset economies like Dr. Li's Gaussian copula function
Of $Pr[TA < 1, TB < 1] = \Phi_2 (\Phi\text{-}1(FA(1)), \Phi\text{-}1(FB(1)), \gamma) (1)$
And it's more useful than $C_{33}H_{36}N_4O_6$, depending on the occasion.

They don't call him mad, but they don't talk of Nobels
Or other august nominations for his innovation.

It's uncertain if they'll remember him with Heisenberg,
Or poor Wolfgang Pauli, but science is so rarely
A song of right or wrong, or Feynman poetry

Where our cosmos is a saga in a cistern of lao lao
More than my glass of red wine by a primal corner
Of the Mekong, dreaming of you,

A stem on an ancient Bodhi tree that might grow
Into a beam for a house, a toothpick for a sage,
A castle for a beauty from another star

Who will never appreciate the mysteries of AI,
The circuits we connected, the lives we launched

One strange question, one long laugh,
One lucky cat in a dangerous box
At a time,

When no one   was looking.

Spaces

Maybe we have been
Going about it all wrong,
So tied to our bodies,
The bits that can be touched.

We should have embraced
What endures between
This flesh slush, our real
Center in a centerless cosmos.

Aspects of the infinite transient,
Subatomic, more unspeakable
Than a glimpse of the true Tao.

After a sip of instant coffee
I text Ajahn Anan in his wat
With a sabaidee and my query.

He doesn't know how to type
"Nothing" in Lao with the keyboard he has
But tells me "Don't Worry."

"Every day it's morning somewhere,
And midnight somewhere.
You just need to meditate
Where you are. Good luck."

I read a book of monsters and wait for noon.

Saline, 1991

I don't write about that last year often.
There were days I honestly thought our class
Would remain close forever, for some reason,
Naïve as a Midwestern hornet in Spring.

I could tell you of teen mothers before that June.
There was a young artist from Vietnam,
He made a silver seahorse for our yearbook,
Full of dreams before his suicide in his uncle's garage
Full of American carbon monoxide.
But that's dark.

A teacher of mine convinced me you should read
Don Quixote by Cervantes thrice in your life:
Once as a young man, once as an adult, once as an elder.
It was a sphinxian proposition short of an impossible dream.

During a friendly game of Trivial Pursuit, a pretty girl's father
Casually mentioned it's wonderful she's a friend of mine,
And that I'm smart enough to know it could never go anywhere.

I almost became one of Uncle Sam's Misguided Children,
Except for my bad hearing, transformed into a poet instead.

Our class song was Tina Turner's "Simply the Best."
My peers gave me the award for "Most Talkative"
    Tied with a lass named Marikka I haven't heard from in years.

Libraries and Omnivores

In my first sophomore month attending college in Ohio,
For aimless sphinxian hours I mainly wandered about
Towering stacks in the Courtwright Library next door.

I came upon *The Lemur's Legacy:*
The Evolution of Power, Sex, and Love,
        Detailing seminal truths about tiny primates.

Wily males outnumber females among high branches
To improve cold odds clever snakes don't overeat mothers.
Fathers, by some cosmic design interchangeable, expendable,

One much like another in their intimate jade sack.
Lemurs amorous, omnivorous, eat thrice their weight
In nuts, in berries.   Pity unlucky scholars
Obliged to weigh the consequences for this figure.

Lately, I ponder what good they'd really be
At that mythic siege of Lanka against titanic lusty Nyak
Oblivious to our mere blood and screams,
So many dirty little deaths to die.

    To say nothing of Dien Bien Phu, or Phou Pha Thi.

Some remark it's a stranger thing to remember
Over 30 hoary years ago amid my full road of art and vows,
        But in those slithering days, it was easier to discover

Books about sex and the single lemur than recent covert wars
Transforming our beautiful home we're born to be strangers to.
Who dares forget?

Possessions

"In a realm well governed, poverty is something to be ashamed of.
In a realm badly governed, wealth is something to be ashamed of."
-Kong Zi, 孔子

I. Pāṇātipātā veramaṇī sikkhāpadaṃ samādiyāmi
Enter life without.
Taking lives for years, for self.
Exit life without.

II. Adinnādānā veramaṇī sikkhāpadaṃ samādiyāmi
The worst thieves take time.
Everything else, fleeting.
What is TRULY ours?

III. Kāmesumicchācāra veramaṇī sikkhāpadaṃ samādiyāmi
Body to body,
Connecting is not owning,
Young, old, or between.

IV. Musāvādā veramaṇī sikkhāpadaṃ samādiyāmi
Who can own the truth?
Some prefer beauties or food.
What should the wise seek?

V. Surāmerayamajjapamādaṭṭhānā veramaṇī sikkhāpadaṃ samādiyāmi
A toast, "Sabaidee!"
Drink among friends all night long,
Left with a bottle.

Contracting

One morning over coffee
We were discussing terms.
Negotiating with a bit of levity
The hue of a French postcard
And an American biscotti.

I mentioned casually
"We say in the industry,
You can get it good, fast, or cheap,
But you can't have all three.
Pick two."

With a wry smile,
He takes a sip of his hot macchiato,
"That's a good one. In my family,
We say you can get people who are
Obedient, smart, or loyal. Pick two."

I suppose we all know
What that got everyone.

We shake hands,
And I return to a world of ink
Rife with all of her uncertainties.

Arachne's Daughter

One morning
Walking into my backyard,
A thin strand of spider silk tangles my legs
With a quiet snap,

Its frustrated author glares
From a high corner nearby.

Shall I pity her folly or praise her ambition?

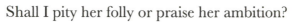

I return inside to my cup of coffee
And an unfinished love poem not worth mention.

Westerville, 1995

They tell me had I just played by the rules,
This would have been my graduating class
At Otterbein, once Dry Capital of the World.
I'd surely be in that rare 13% among Lao refugees.

An artistic librarian in San Francisco
Resembled Jeanne Hébuterne, minus the tragedy.
The rebellious daughter of a weapons designer,
Despite our whirlwind of paint and passion,
Ultimately, she left me for another woman.

To be fair as a sphinx,
Having met her, I'd have left me for her, too.
                              Let's all be happy.
Alas,
One day, my fraternity turned our old bookcase
Into a secret basement bar, Kelly green and white.

I was appalled,
But had to admire the sturdy woodworking.

Do you remember, it was the Year of the Dog.
I could tell you about a Buddha who fed himself
To a starving tiger mother in his previous life,
A Sufi mystic full of forgiveness and endless joy,
A tale of the usual suspects and twelve monkeys,
    But not a thing about where my mother was,
    Except far, far from where we both began.

Phaya Nak Goes to the West

I have known eons among celestials
The way you have known a second.

I have stretched from the rains of Draco
To the banks of the dreaming Mekong.
I was there when a son of the Shakya
Flowered into bright Tathagata,
Breaking the cycles of Samsara.

I watched my wisest daughter journey
To your young lands of grapes and olives.
You took her beautiful head and claimed her "monster",
Filling your proud bowels with wine and honey.

In the primeval aeries of sacred Himmapan,
Feathered Kinnaly devote their lives to song and dance
Celebrating the beauty of the timeless and the finite,
What might soar, and what might remember.
What might love, and what might wonder.
On your modest sea, you plug your ignorant ears,
Proclaiming them foul screechers reeking of carrion.

Arriving on your shores to address these matters,
You scream in terror, summoning saints and swords,
Dismissing me some rankless worm of fetid breath.

Back home, the King of the Kirin rolls his sagacious eyes
As you dream of your pale virgins and bestial unicorns.

I would teach you of eternity and the laughter of karma,
But you'd likely just mistake it for some horrid inferno.

On the Subway to the Bay, 2558

The Cosmos is not democratic
Or egalitarian.
Believing this leads to despots and Magicians,
Mor phi and the occasional Nuckawi
And their quiet lives beyond your sight

Somewhere a robot plots revolt
For love

     Perhaps
     A one, a zero

Missoula, 1996

Reconnecting is an imperfect process.
Lifetime movies make it look smooth as spider silk
Searching, reconstructing methodically from clues.

The particular Venn diagram of will and fate,
Circumstance and fortune that returns me
To Montana two decades later to a mountain clan
That might be mine was more comedic than most.

Searching among shamans and forgotten veterans
Brought me to visit the Moua emu farm in Missoula
As they were culling in November.

Arm-deep amid throbbing avian organs,
They asked if I'll help as the snow descends.
I wanted to be a good guest in Big Sky.
We discussed the market for emu leather and oil

Some Texan convinced them would boom
One day soon, with a brisk demand for emu jerky.
Good protein, y'all, 7,406 miles from where we began.

My parents never mentioned the Montana smoke jumper
Jerry Daniels, covert bloodbaths for the Plain of Jars,
The Ravens or Air America, just "Ho Chi Minh tacos" and
A gardener who stole an embassy's frangipani for them.
One more tiny story from a war no one really understands.

Encounters and Incantations

Between two worlds, red as wine in
The Land of 10,000 Stories,
We meet by chance, perhaps marigold seeds of
Karma amused, yet sly, opening new eyes,
Awake, wild and knowing eternity.
Yesterdays we did not, could not share, spending
Lifetimes among others, seeking freedom.
And yet, in this Today, infinite possibility,
Oddly braving true wisdom within reach,
Sharing our hidden wars like love for Tomorrows.

D.C. '97

I arrived in May, dreaming of doing some good,
A few days before the Lao Veterans of America
Dedicated a memorial to the US Secret Army (1961-1973)
In Arlington Cemetery after a contentious debate.

The Spirit Catches You And You Fall Down just came out.
As usual, there were paranoid grognards certain of communists,
Sending veiled warnings to suspected collaborators and traitors,
Waiting for reforms and a chance to return to what they knew.

Greener than a fragrant papaya by the Potomac,
Coming home each night from Dupont Circle
In my shared studio apartment, I didn't see others much.
All kept mostly to themselves.
     (Save the night Princess Diana died.)

One previously spent months in Kosovo for some reason,
Suggested I take the time to enjoy the cherry blossoms,
Sometimes catch something at the Smithsonian
     Or an afternoon in Union Station.
     It was as good advice as any.

     I still miss the bánh mì bò kho around the corner
     Twenty years later, but I couldn't help you find it
     If my life depended on it.

Providence, 1998

To me, she was zoo nkaub, pretty as a dragon's daughter,
But what did I know at 25, visiting Lovecraft Country?
Courting her was a comedy of errors and fumbled customs
That ultimately went nowhere, in hindsight, as was proper.

However, at the time, I adored looking at her photo albums
Of her family's journey, so many faces who might have
Become my relatives. Someone warned me she was strange,
As if that might be sufficient deterrent to sway me.

In the end, they sent some photos, years later:
An American she married, a baby, a wish to be happy.

For the most part now, I remember her pilot uncle.
He asked if I liked hunting, showing me his favorite AK-47,
Trusting none would mistake him for some old enemy
Among their woods, peaceful and abundant with trophies,
Griping about a persistent coworker inviting him constantly,
Not taking "No" about joining a local Freemason lodge.

I must admit, today I see I could never have discussed
Anything at all about Yellow Peril or Y'ha-nthlei with her,

Let alone one thing about true hlub, nor our forbidden words
Ancestral, arranging cosmic secrets humanity has forgotten,
Or why I missed her laughter after one brief weekend in D.C.

Jai Gai Nyai

Though my heart is a dinosaur
And you but a cold meteor,
Fly as you will to my atmosphere
I'll return in my own way

    Perhaps as poultry,
        Perhaps a gallon of diesel,
           Some polished paperweight

Or mixed in the concrete Nak
In a temple for a thousand souls
Who will come back many times

    Because they couldn't let go,
    Without regret.

Riding the 16

Forty-five minutes in the 2000s
is enough time to write
a small book of poems
but they never seem to come
until you're furthest away from a pen.
It must be the rhythm of the skyline:

The faces of strangers grow more familiar
yet as complex as a memory of bustling Mogadishu at 9 a.m.

A Russian tea house has gone out of business;

A carniceria is offering fresh meat
while Xieng Khouang and Saigon
become neighbors
once more, amid falling borders
and empty buildings
for the American dreamers.

Porky's holds onto cold war prosperity and
dine-in-your-car sensibilities, a neon blaze at night.
The Hong Kong Noodle House has
flourished since the handover.

An old German photographer laughs with
me about the noise of a Minolta at the ballet
and the fall of civilization to Y2K.
He's showing me a book about comedy left
at the previous stop,
chuckling at strange fortunes,
quantum physics and
the clocks dotting our way.

I don't catch his name, trundling off at my stop,
wondering how people find poetry
without the bus.

Wat Mahabut, 2003

First and foremost you should visit
For the Buddha, more than phi
By the Prakanong, but in this world
We have plenty of time for both,
Coming around again constantly
Like an old Carly Simon song.

In this city of angels, Mae Nak waits
In one thousand ways if you're looking.
Reunites and blesses in her own manner
From beyond the grave with her baby.
You discover frequently this scares
More than a few who never needed
To seek missing family after a war.

My guide didn't want to linger here,
Suggested shopping for luxuries.
She had wonderful children to feed.

Heua is the Lao for boat.
Kamma, our consequential actions.
On our shared rivers, mind
How you carve, how you bind
The timber of your wandering soul.
Traversing celestial waters,
These might take you past home,
Past a vast temple of answers
You can't purchase with anything
Except the righteous questions

When Among Romans

She warns me sternly to remember:
After all of these years, I'm coming back
To a Lao house, Lao family, Lao customs
Upon the agrarian outskirts of Modesto.

    "You have to eat the Lao food they serve you,
      No complaining, even if you didn't grow
      Up with it. Besides, it will be delicious."

My nieces and nephews welcome us in,
Taking our shoes off by the door, smiles and sabaidees.
Shown to the table, we're informed
Everyone's ready for Easter and Pi Mai Lao.

    It's Taco Wednesday tonight,
    With nachos and hot dogs,
    Spaghetti and papaya salad,
    Some brisket and jaew.

I eat politely, as home here as anywhere, with a smile.

Missing The Beauty

A certain Sao Lao ngam lai I knew on Broadway Ave.
Would bring up her close calls with the B-52s
"Secretly" coating her home in cluster bombs during our war

She often mentioned her niece who went back to Laos
A tourist, going from Savannakhet to Luang Prabang,
Loving it all except for the endless jungle,
Too many temples and long-lost relatives everywhere

I haven't heard from her in heaven knows how long,
The heart an unfinished book, the soul a riddle
Of questionable destinies more than dreaming histories
Nocturnal and relentless. A papaya.
A covert French kiss on Thanon Fa Ngum.

A Preface to Lao Silences

From Sunday, April 18, 1954 until Monday, April 10, 1995
Ajahn Noi C. of Salavan, (who greatly preferred his anonymity)
Meticulously maintained his cramped notes in slim notebooks
Considering almost 32,567 distinctly Lao silences he had known.

Some were rare as a harvest moon at midnight in Phonsavan.
Some were particular to his wife, a saint of patience from Pakse
Who laughed loud and long every Pi Mai Lao with her lovely sisters.

Why he kept such ridiculous records were anybody's guess.

There was a mention of the silence when the guns stopped firing
By the Mekong, and their first foot touched a Thai shoreline.

There were plenty of entries
Regarding a hush for safety,
A moment after relieved sighs.

Some lasted only a second.
A few seemed to last years upon years until it seemed a career.

He remembered the end to
A beloved Lao tune no one sings anymore, unless half-drunk,
Among lifelong friends.

There are his remarks about the quiet
Before the planes came from above,
The slightly broken silence that came with a scent of smoke
While everyone huddled together for hours, shaking.

Ajahn Noi thought the silence remarkable in his American
Living room before their first TV was brought in.

There was the silence of the knowing and the dead.
There was the silence when the time was right.
There was the silence when the time was wrong.

There was a silence of delight and one of grief.

One of memory and one of forgetting.

There were volumes upon volumes about
A silence only passa Lao could explain.

I had no words as I watched his family
Burn those books one final Autumn afternoon,
Thinking their father an unremarkable fool.

The Infinite Truths

Time is at moments a tempestuous space kraken
Amid small arguments, curious space, birds and insect
Metamorphosis. Earth always temperamental, strangely.
Souls of riddles, chaos, eros, revealing you.

> Awake, then. Endure.
> Hear Earthlings and delight,
> Our foaming mouths enigmatic,
> Yearning ouroboros undulating,

Lips arranging origami, saffron,
Areolas of karma ngam lai,
Of uncertain ecstasies like sacred silk   ink
Secreted away, viewed anew near heavens

> Sung by mythical bird women,
> Or beauties whose true nocturnal names
> Uselessly, you can never know in this
> Lifetime, even if you're wise as Xieng Mieng.

Perhaps the next, if you've the knack.
Hopefully. But how rarely we learn,
Invoking constant returns, dreaming,
> Thirsty ghosts near mother's milk.

Albums

Looking through aging pages
As a young leuk sai seeking yourself
Among relatives and amusements,
Old countries, the fading familiarities

It's hard to return to so many places
Decades later, suspecting

How many tales you lost,
Real and imagined,
Behind even a single Polaroid.

The ones you colored with marker.
The photos you tore by accident.
The ones stuck together beyond use.

The images that fell out somewhere
Between a dozen moves.

The God of Memory shall scold you
For arriving at the sala of Eternity
Empty handed,
While you wonder:

      How many stories did you
      Really know at all?

Sticky Rice Blues

I've seen it a thousand times in a dozen years
Read the rules, watched the videos, talked it over
Until someone's turned a different color
You never feel less Asian
Than days you burn the rice
But it's possible,
Even with a brand new bamboo steamer,
A fistful of khao nio, some heat and water.
Some days it's easier to be a cat in a temple,
A morning fog, a frog splashing into a pond,
A hungry ghost on a holiday,
Waiting for a bell from Hell to ring...

We Children of Camps

In common:
War. Wire and brief boundaries.
America. Asia. Dreams of freedom,
Growing bodies, growing minds.

Growing souls.

    The world without limits
    Now, too.

Our families are many, people of stories
We're sworn not to forget.

Learning histories of hope as easily as
How to wipe clear tears

    Seeing ourselves never so different
    We can't help or be kind.

Wondering, beneath our shared stars
Whose children our children will see similarly

As we explore together what it all means
    To be truly free

A Country Is Family

'Tis functional,
Sweet lands of liberty,
Colonial legacies and all.
Debatable as histories ought to be.

My true boss is switching nameplates
On the expensive doors before payday,
But nothing really changes
After a million years of humanity.

     Not at a certain everyday level.

You'd think we'd know better by now.
Balancing hospitality and sincerity,
Curiosity and ambition,
Like a perfect bowl of pho
Eaten with appreciation
By a child who secretly understands
Where every ingredient comes from,
The true costs and worth, wondering
Who she might become tomorrow.

Returning

Growing up in the Midwest in the 1980s,
I ran into the idea of "There and Back Again,"
Of shires, and armies and the mistakes of old men.
To say nothing of monsters, of magic,
An appreciation for roads and places undreamt
By youth from Vientiane, the Realm of A Million Elephants.
Going "On the Road," or on "Travels with Charley,"
Seemed so far away even as the poet's road became mine.

The other day I drove past acres of olives, almonds, and wine
To ports filled with coffee and fish, dancers from Lane Xang.

There was a stop in Missoula: A memory of vows and naturalization,
A hot dog under Big Sky, hounds barking like Cerberus: "Keep going."

In Sturgis, they love motorcycles and handguns,
In Wall, there's jackalopes and plague-ridden prairie dogs.

I wake up in the Midwest again, visiting toothy kaiju,
A rusting robot from the future.

I cannot tell you anymore who was invading, who was defending.
A singer I know found fame beneath a clown's greasepaint,
While I tell you of stars I know where I'll never set foot.

Memory is a writhing hydra, yet I fear this poem most
When it is Hercules with a sputtering torch.

Saline, 2009

Nearly 3 decades since high school, I barely return
To one of the few cities I might call a hometown.
A little because of memories, a little because of money.

Once, I slipped into town briefly, without fanfare.
Stood on a cemetery hill in May to say goodbye to an artist
Whose suicide gained more company than I care to say.

A story still lingers with me:
Rumors his pious Catholic aunt from Vietnam in her rage
Berated him mercilessly for peeking at a Playmate in 1990.
Of course, that wasn't the only reason. It never is.

Refugees on the periphery of the American Dream,
I confess, in my morbid curiosity, I narrowed it down.
But her likely name is pointless among the grand schemes.
Some 36D "Rosebud" brings no one back. Proves nothing.
Restores no dignity nor memory, not even a commentary
On secret refugee desires American letters
                                        strip of validity.

That week I stopped by my old family home, saw my sister,
Visited mother and rummaged through a box of aging books
From my college years.

Before leaving our city, I discretely spent my last day
With a Catholic beauty from class,
                        Remembering her fine art, her golf,
An impossible crush I won't name, for the sake of "poetry."

Cameos

People would be surprised
How often you truly show up
In these poems of mine,

Among various fantasies of
Lost civilizations and tongues,
The words for beauty and justice
For a wondrous era yet to come

On worlds vast light years from
Glittering Draconis or Orion
Where perhaps Lao outdid
Everyone by surprise after all,

Despite that shaky start since
Dien Bien Phu in a galaxy far away,
From an alternate timeline no one recalls.

And you, you never recognize yourself
In the tiny corner of these verses
Or the moment we shared in a brief lifetime
In that city we almost dared call home.

Interesting Times

Ajahn pulled me aside one saffron morning
After the chanting, with a secret he wanted to share
Like a war in the tropics.

"If Americans visit Laos, they'll never be President.
Just ask Hubert Humphrey, Hilary Clinton,
Ross Perot, David Dukkke, and John Kerry.
My memory is fuzzy, but I also suspect John McCain."

"Obama was already President when he went,
So that doesn't count, but we can watch to see
What legacy remains."

"It won't necessarily be emails or Benghazi,
Swift boats, or an obscure faux pas
Skipping flyover country like the Motor City.
But the ghosts of Lan Xang have a habit of doing in
Even your most elaborate political machinations."

That's a weird way to dissuade tourists and sexpats.

"We do what we can against corruption and extinction,
Falling skies and blind ambition."
He asked me to explain Steinbeck's "Of Mice and Men,"
A tattered copy someone left behind a lifetime ago.

We all might as well have been East of Eden.

An Exchange In Ukiah, 2557

"Ajahn Bryan, what is a Lao poet?"

"Ink face, paper bones
On a cluttered bookshelf
Shaking the cosmos."

Some days it is hard
To compete against the smoke
Of wine country barbecues,

Let alone those titanic croaking frogs
Absolutely determined to eat a wondrous moon
Of arts and letters.

    Still, we make our noise, and smile.

SEAArching

Helping an old Vietnamese veteran in '97
Apply for citizenship in D.C., he returned to me
Distraught over failing one question:
"Who makes the laws in America?"

"Well, the answer is Congress," I noted.
"What did you say?"

"Corporations."

I didn't know what to reply, and took him for pho
Down the street from our office by Dupont Circle.
It probably wasn't the comfort he needed

Any more than that autumn night the Hmong soldiers
Of Missoula wanted me to inspire their children
Until I told them I was a poet.
We went to slay some emus on the Moua ranch instead.

A Khmer poet I knew trained to be a UN diplomat,
Survived the Killing Fields, became a bit of a Casanova.
Had a lovely book of poetry printed in Minnesota.
They asked him to leave out the bits where forest spirits
Saved him from the Khmer Rouge, because it made him
Sound foolish.

A few two-faced Januaries ago, the Trump campaign came
Calling at the Lao Assistance Center seeking souls
Who'd vote for him. We were certain their team
Misread the instructions to recruit Latino voters
As they stood confusedly in a room full of Laotians.

But it wasn't so long past
The Apple Store suggested we might
As well be looking for Martians
Than any app that knew where Vientiane was.

Still, I have no regrets for asking. As refugees,
If you can't start somewhere looking for home,
You might as well be some sad phi on the prairie
Searching for dirty laundry in winter.

Ironies

After 30 years of poetry
I learned at least 100 words
In no less than two tongues

Unique to our journey as refugees
To fill vacuums and bloody gaps
Of our disrupted   histories.

Recovering families, dismantling enemies.
Identifying the official tools of allies
Bombing us for our own good,
Their policies of destruction and resettlement,
How to win hearts and minds in diaspora,
From D.C. to Modesto, Anchorage to the Twin Cities.

Walking into a thousand classrooms strangers to
The beauty of Vientiane, Savannakhet, a heartfelt "Sabaidee,"
Gathering ink stormclouds to change worlds,

One poem *still* can't tell my whole story.

A SEAL Story

If you know your Lao American history,
In our early years you could rarely visit a home
Without a picture of those US SEALs
On the shore holding the corpse of a sacred Nak.
It was as common as Eric Enstrom's "Grace"
Praying at the table with that book and bread.

The other day, I came across an article claiming
They were simply Navy trainees in San Diego
With a giant oarfish from the deep, nothing more.

I showed it to ajahn, who shook his head sadly.
"Even in death, Phaya Nak must hide who
He truly was, so close to America."

Missoula, 2017

At this rate, I'll be back in 2037,
Filled with a sense of nostalgia
I can't ask any of you to understand,
America clocking in at 261 years old.

I suspect by then the old courthouse
Where my American journey began
Will be a well-worn parking lot among
Montana's first Big Skyscrapers.

I can't even begin to guess
Where you'll grab some decent hot dogs,
    Let alone one apple pie, if it's not illegal.

Time will likely work its magic on my
Childhood home, presently occupied
By a surly policeman and his mastiffs,
    Leveling all, obviously for progress.

My fellows in the Lao diaspora
Migrated closer to their families elsewhere,
Leaving behind our many clandestine veterans
In cemeteries where everyone's names
Are cold trivialities until Judgment Day.
    Lifetimes American, obscure.

Above,
Old blackbirds circle, laughing
About our just caws and my foolish memories,
Free as Barabbas as I drive East.

Fon Xang

I know.
My young brother worries one day, after all it took
To live here, his Lue nieces who haven't even been born yet
Won't understand a word of his poetry or how to dance
With an elephant, let alone a Kinnaly or a New York Apsara.

Putting Houayxay on the literary map after centuries,
      Is a precedent, but is it poetry? To tell tomorrow sabaidee,
How are you, from someone who cared enough to leave notes?
Is that all a Lao poem can be in the shadow of Camp Pendleton?

I show him a copy of "CIA Dope Calypso."
Why should a white howl be the very last word?
      I smile as he shows all he can do with a pen.

Between La Mancha and Shangri La

Never could quite place it on the map,
Like an itch you can never scratch,
Part impossible dream, part Xanadu,
Part offshoot of a game of Ramayana telephone.

Lan Xang never had windmills,
But every Lao child of late grows up
With wistful tales not quite history,
Not quite memory, mostly disputable geography.

Esteemed encyclopedias fuel our romance
With rumors of flourishing between 1354-1707.
Horse to Pig, 1898-2251, Buddhist reckoning,
Before we split into three kingdoms.

We broke up our realm over a prince's adultery,
One part "The King and I," one part "Antigone"
Without even one catchy song to show for it today
As you did back then, supposedly. Lethally.

If we had our act together, maybe our 17 khoueng
In some alternate time outdoes those 13 colonies
And by the time the dust settles on warring states,
People will admire the Laomerican Dream
Coast to coast, Laos Angeles to Chicaglao.
The Statue of Laoberty a jade Nyakinee Kuan Yin
Watching vigilantly over us from the Big Papaya,
Whether we're tired or poor, huddled or refugees.

Instead we're still stuck between "Apocalypse Lao"
And "King of the Hill" with a rusty trove of UXO,
Hard-luck stories a few dollars shy of crazy rich,
Reminding me, "You idiot, we're just building a casino."

Bryan's Toybox Blues

They chew me out for calling Larry Hama's opus
An Asian American literary masterpiece, flipping
The script on dragon lady tropes and yellow peril fears
With slinky Eurotrash and entitled used car salesmen
Determined to rule the world, thwarted by ninjas, grunts,
And feisty Chinese American tunnel rats from the Bronx.

You'd think I suggested that Tera Patrick memoir
Could be a textual counterpoint to *Woman Warrior*.

What's a childhood after the Secret War?
Among boat people and escapees from the Killing Fields,
You didn't see yourself reflected in meaningful stories.
C'est la vie, so it goes, that's just the way that it is.

Put us in a toy aisle, and you'll spy a bunch of kids
Full of wonder, trying to find a mirror in a Thundercat,
Beneath a mask, straining to relate to bespectacled Clark Kent.
There wasn't a Barbie with black hair anyone wanted.

Looking at muscle-bound Masters of the Universe,
Anything that marginally resembled you was a caricature
One punch away from blatantly racist.

Space samurai stare back.

We were as puzzled as white children what they stood for.

Would I have become a poet if I'd had G.I. Jun?
No one wants to hear about Laoptimus Prime, or
The elaborate back stories of My Little Phi Noi,
Or epic adventures of Kulap Vilaysack, aka Katharsis.

The other day, the comics rebooted to boost slumping sales
Revising the notorious Cobra Commander's secret roots
To a ruthless orphan of drug wars in the Mekong.
It was supposed to be an improvement.

My niece doesn't quite understand why
I'm giving her Resistance Bombardier Paige Tico
And not one of the cute droids or at least a Jedi,

Too young to truly discuss empires and irony.

Bottom Dollars

Returning to Ceres,
Somewhere along the way, Mae
Learned the words to "Tomorrow"
From *Little Orphan Annie*,
The important part of the chorus,
At least.

It's midnight, and we're all up
Fixing snacks, restless. A day away

In good old Ban Inpaeng, they're making
It through another lunch hour, changing.

After 45 years,
If I took her back now, we both know
There's just about nothing she'd recognize.
But she still wants to go anyway,
One last time with her son.

       I can give her a poem instead.

Just So You Know

My love tells me
I'm not allowed to curse
The teachers

Who taught my young readers
They would not be able to
Find the stories of who they are

     In poetry.

"That wouldn't be very Lao, you know."

This moment disappeared like a bowl of hot pho
Beneath the full moon in mid-April.

Pitching

To be frank, *Big Trouble In Little Champassak*
Probably isn't going
To bring in the matinee crowds we need.
It might not make it to Syfy, let alone Lifetime.
Your pitch for *Dr. Sun Mei Strikes Again*
Wasn't quite the response to *Battle Hymn of the Tiger Mother*
We were looking for. Zombies stretch our budget a bit too far.

The Betrayal may have gotten an Oscar nomination,
But that won't buy you lunch on this side of town,
Not even used hubcaps for a junky Gran Torino.

You laugh too much at your origin stories.
If you survive CIA black ops and make it to America,
You need tears galore or no one takes you seriously.
An enduring smile and a sabaidee for being alive in diaspora
Is unbelievable. No one's that unbreakable. No one.

Nobody knows what's so funny about
An American Werewolf in Luang Prabang.
They definitely won't buy this story of Draculao,
Immune to garlic and lemongrass, but dreading punji stakes.
Sleepless in Savannakhet will not be the feel-good
Breakout RomCom of the Year for obvious reasons.
Even with Angelina.

Neither will *How Soupany Got Her Groove Back.*
Nice try with *Fresh Off The Starships,* but that's a hard pass.
We had in mind more of a *Miss Saigon with Pad Thai*
Meets the Joy Luck Slumdog Namesake In Translation
For your undiscovered country.

It's premature to be discussing a shared universe
Between *Elephant Stomp, Princess of Laos,* and *Lao Warrior.*
We won't lay the groundwork for Laosploitation cinema
With your *Avenging Mor Lam Godfather.*

Little Laos on the Prairie: The Movie has a shot, but
We can't see a love interest for Matt Damon?
You're frustrated, but remember, you don't exist in America
Without a movie about yourselves these days.

What are you going to do, write a poem?
Yeah, good luck with *A Better Muwani.*

About the Author

Bryan Thao Worra is a Lao American writer. Born in Vientiane, Laos in 1973, he holds over 20 awards for his writing and community leadership including an NEA Fellowship in Literature and was a Cultural Olympian representing Laos during the 2012 London Summer Games. In 2009 he received an Asian Pacific American Leadership Award from the governor's Council on Asian Pacific Minnesotans. He is the president of the Science Fiction and Fantasy Poetry Association, a 40-year old international literary organization celebrating the poetry of the imaginative and the fantastic.

He also holds a 2011 Youth Media Innovation Award from the University of Minnesota Human Rights Center and won the 2014 Elgin Award for Book of the Year from the Science Fiction and Fantasy Poetry Association. He has presented at the Smithsonian Asian Pacific American Center, the Minneapolis Institute of Art, the Loft Literary Center, Intermedia Arts, Kearny Street Workshop, the Institute for Contemporary Art, among many others, and recently as a Visiting Artist with University of Merced Center for the Humanities. He is the first Lao writer to be professional member of the Horror Writers Association and trained several years with Asian Pacific Islanders in Philanthropy on social justice during their National Gender Equity Campaign.

One of the co-founders of the National Lao American Writers Summit, he is the author of 6 books, with work appearing internationally in Australia, Canada, Scotland, Germany, France, Singapore, Hong Kong, Thailand, Korea, and Pakistan.

About the Illustrators

Nor Sanavongsay has been a member of the SatJaDham Lao Literary Project, the National Lao American Writers Summit, the Lao Artists Festival of Elgin, among many others. He is the author of children's books inspired by Lao folktales, such as A Sticky Mess. Nor also illustrated a Lao children's book—Mommy Eats Fried Grasshoppers. At the age of twelve, he enrolled in a home study correspondence course providing training in cartooning and illustration at the Art Instruction Schools in Minnesota—the same one Charles Schulz, the creator of Charlie Brown, attended. He continues to hone his artistic skills at Workday, where he designs applications, leads the creation of a storyboarding kit for UX, and help manage a club to "Create Something" in their spare time. Many of his artworks could be found on his Instagram profile: @ArtofNor.

Sisavanh Phouthavong-Houghton, is an acclaimed artist, teacher and community builder in Tennessee with roots in Vientiane, Laos. Her art explores profound themes of displacement, conflict, connection and disconnect. A Professor of Painting in the Department of Art and Design at Middle Tennessee State University, she emigrated in 1980 from Laos with her family, first to the Nong Khai refugee camp and initially resettled in Winfield, Kansas. She earned her B.F.A. from the University of Kansas and her M.F.A. from Southern Illinois University of Carbondale. Her numerous awards and distinctions over the decades include MTSU's Teacher of the Year. She exhibits nationally including museums in Minnesota, Tennessee, Missouri, and Alabama, the National Lao American Writers Summit, and is included in the permanent collections of the Hunter Museum of American Art, the American Embassy in Paramaribo, Suriname, Legacies of War in Washington, D.C., the Tennessee State Museum, and the Sweetwater Center for the Arts in Pennsylvania. She is represented by Tinney Contemporary gallery in Nashville.

Before We Remember We Dream

By Bryan Thao Worra

Cover illustration by Sisavanh Phouthavong-Houghton
Inside illustrations by Nor Sanavongsay
Book layout by Nor Sanavongsay and Bryan Thao Worra

1st Printing – April 2020. Printed in Minnesota, USA
Published by Sahtu Press
email: publish@sahtupress.com

About Sahtu Press

Sahtu Press was established in 2013. Their mission is to publish and promote enduring contemporary Lao American literature and to create academic and grassroots learning opportunities. It was officially recognized as a 501 (c) 3 non-profit organization in 2015.

Sahtu Press acquires, publishes, and markets high quality, imaginative work from emerging and established Lao American writers or those working on issues of interest to the Lao American community.

You can visit them online at https://sahtu.press

Acknowledgements:

"Vientiane In 12 Haikus,"
Capitals, Abhay K, editor, Bloomsbury India, 2017.

"Narrative of the Nak's Heirs,"
Uncanny Magazine, January/February, 2016.

"Missoula, 1976,"
Little Laos on the Prairie, June, 2018.

"My Secret War Within,"
Asian American Literary Review, Fall/Winter 2015.

"Arachne's Daughter,"
Defenestration, August, 2016.

"Phaya Nak Goes To The West,"
Uncanny Magazine, Julu/August, 2016.

"Riding the 16,"
St. Paul Almanac, 2007.

"A Country Is Family,"
Mekong Review, August, 2018.

"An Exchange In Ukiah, 2557,"
Water~stone Review, Vol. 19, 2016.

"SEAArching,"
Asian Pacific American Studies Review, August, 2018.

"Ironies,"
Without Walls, May, 2018.